50 WAYS
TO
LOSE YOUR
GLASSES

50 WAYS
TO
LOSE YOUR
GLASSES

WARBY PARKER

Illustrations by John Lee

 hachette
BOOKS *NEW YORK BOSTON*

Hachette Books
Hachette Book Group
1290 Avenue of the Americas
New York, NY 10104

www.HachetteBookGroup.com

Printed in the United States of America

RRD-C

First Edition: October 2015
10 9 8 7 6 5 4 3 2 1

Hachette Books is a division of Hachette Book Group, Inc.

The publisher is not responsible for websites (or their content) that are not owned by the publisher.

Library of Congress Cataloging-in-Publication Data has been applied for.

ISBN: 978-0-3163-4484-5 (Hardcover)/ISBN: 978-0-3163-4482-1 (ebook)

50 WAYS
TO
LOSE YOUR
GLASSES

Pickpocket

Shark

The great outdoors

Distraction

Sleepwalking

Cat burglar

Time travel

Garbage disposal

Trading floor

Advanced yoga

Accident

Airbag

Goat

Poker

Alien encounter

Tantrum

Anti-gravity chamber

Booby trap

Cardio

Pogo stick

Coney Island Cyclone

Centrifugal force

Contact sports

Friendly competition

Drone

Ghost

Team-building exercise

Her majesty

Rodeo

A night at the opera

Magic

Landfill

Mega sneeze

Karaoke

Man's best friend

Manhole

Pratfall

Seismic activity

Raptor

Housework

Spontaneous combustion

Elves

Practical joke

Subway performance

Swamp monster

Mosh pit

Stick-up

Promotion

Limbo

Momentary lapse

ABOUT THE AUTHOR

Warby Parker is a transformative lifestyle brand with a lofty objective: to offer designer eyewear at a revolutionary price while leading the way for socially conscious businesses. Founded in 2010 and named after two characters in an early Jack Kerouac journal, Warby Parker believes in creative thinking, smart design, and doing good in the world. For every pair of glasses sold, a pair is distributed to someone in need.

warbyparker.com

ABOUT THE ILLUSTRATOR

John Lee is a bespectacled illustrator from Memphis, Tennessee. He attended the Illustration as Visual Essay program at the School of Visual Arts, and currently lives in Brooklyn, New York.

johnleedraws.com

MORE GREAT BOOKS BY WARBY PARKER!

Stay tuned for these forthcoming titles by Warby Parker—coming soon to a bookstore near you.

Laserdiscs: The Golden Year

Yoga, Yogurt, Yurts: An Ancient Synergy

Baking with Sawdust

Semi-Colons; Did I Do that Right?

Typos for Hihgly Effective People

How to Skin an Egg and Other Mountain Wisdom

Benjamin Franklin: Unplugged

Intermediate Karate for Beginners

What Your Social Security Number Says About You

1,001 Wild & Crazy Zoning Laws

"Fancy" Math

So You Think You Can Read

My Outhouse, My Rules!

How to Confuse People with Your Words and Actions